pocket gardens

pocket gardens

Contemporary Japanese
Miniature Designs

pocket gardens

Contemporary Japanese
Miniature Designs

Michael Freeman

with
Noriko Sakai
Heidi Kingstone
Yukako Shibata

UNIVERSE

We would like to thank not only the garden designers
and architects whose inspiring work is featured here,
but also the owners and clients, who kindly allowed us to
intrude on their homes, and who for reasons of privacy
prefer to remain anonymous.

First published in the United States of America in 2008 by
UNIVERSE PUBLISHING
A Division of Rizzoli International Publications, Inc.
300 Park Avenue South
New York, NY 10010
www.rizzoliusa.com

2008 2009 2010 2011 2012 / 10 9 8 7 6 5 4 3 2 1

Printed in China
ISBN-13: 978-0-7893-1587-8
Library of Congress Catalog Control Number: 2007934240

Design by Claudia Brandenburg, Language Arts

introduction

Over the centuries, garden design in Japan has evolved into an art form, embodying philosophy, religion, aesthetics, and individual creative expression. One branch is concerned with miniaturization (a goal that extends to many other areas of design in Japan as well), and traditionally the best-known expression of this is the *tsubo-niwa*, a tiny square courtyard garden the size of two tatami mats laid side by side. These gardens are designed not to be walked in, but rather to be seen and admired, or used for contemplation.

Architecture in Japan has evolved as well, but while the form of dwellings and their urban context have changed, the need for gardens remains. Because the size of the living space is, as always, a constraint, miniaturization is a necessity, although one that has in many ways been translated into a virtue. Presented here are fifty-three small garden spaces, all created within the last several years, that bring nature into the houses and apartments of modern Japan.

The traditional *tsubo-niwa* embodied the principle of a microcosm of nature, and while the formal rules for achieving this have been replaced by a variety of approaches, many of them personal, the core of the idea remains. The thoughtful selection of a few elements and their considered composition are common to all the small gardens here, and they succeed in bringing a distillation of nature into dwellings. This suggests ties with the art of bonsai, in which normal species of trees are carefully nurtured and trained to grow as miniatures. But a deeper connection goes further back in history to the Chinese tradition of *penjing*, the art of creating a miniature landscape in a container. On a philosophical level, *penjing* invokes harmony and unity through the interaction of opposites—*yin-yang* in Chinese, *in-yo* in Japanese. These same principles are applied here in these thoughtful modern gardens. At a fundamental level of the harmony of opposites, they bring the restorative powers of nature in symbolic form to the interior environment of a home.

center

In general, the classic interior garden in a Japanese house is a courtyard garden of extremely small dimensions known as *tsubo-niwa*. *Niwa* means garden, and *tsubo* is a traditional area measurement in the *shakkan-ho* system (one of the traditional Japanese measurement systems) equal to two tatami mats laid side by side. Each mat is approximately the area occupied comfortably by a prone figure—usually 35 by 70 inches. The tatami mat was a kind of Japanese version of Le Corbusier's famous Modulor, based on human dimensions and used for area measurement in rooms and in construction.

Two combined make a square approximately 35 square feet in area. The *tsubo-niwa* in the center of a house is essentially a reworking—a miniaturization—of the layout of the courtyard house, a tradition borrowed from China. These small courtyard gardens share with their larger Chinese antecedents two important attributes: they solve the problem of opening the dwelling to the sky while maintaining privacy, and they provide an architectural focus for the entire structure. The house revolves around this central point, and rooms on all four sides face inward to nature.

The courtyard garden traditionally stands at the heart of the Japanese house, with the rooms facing onto it. One of the aims of creating this kind of space, however small, is to combine the feeling of openness with a sense of enclosure. In the words of Kazuyo Sejima and Ryue Nishizawa, the architects who designed this sunken dwelling in the center of Tokyo, the central courtyard serves to "bring the outside into the interior, while at the same time securing privacy for the living space."

What makes the design of this house unique is that most of it is one level below grade, with the minimalist, almost austere garden acting as a light well. Small though it is, the space seems larger, partly thanks to its transparent and translucent walls, and partly because of the height of the excavated area. Decking and a single dogwood comprise the entire garden. The tree was carefully chosen for its soft and delicate lines, which counter the austerity of the space. Walls of glass and translucent polycarbonate reflect and reinforce the centrality of the design. Light entering directly from above is filtered through white-painted steel louvers, which give an added measure of privacy, and also cast a lovely pattern over the garden in the middle of the day.

right: Framed by and reflected in the surrounding windows, a single dogwood occupies the end of the sunken garden.

right: The glow from interior lights filters through translucent polycarbonate panels, emphasizing the dogwood's delicate structure.
facing page: Steel louvers painted white form an open roof above the garden.

Over the centuries, the Japanese have perfected the concept of less is more, as exemplified here. Few places are as tranquil and visually restful as the Zen-inspired garden of Villa Esterio in Kobu, with its bare white walls, white gravel, and sculpted maple, chosen for the deep and intense red color of its leaves in the fall. This is intentionally the only source of color in the otherwise white complex of buildings and courtyards that comprise this wedding center.

Architect Atsushi Kitagawara's concept for this development, which includes a large chapel and numerous reception rooms, was what he calls "Maze and Sky." Its location, Kobu city in Yamanashi prefecture, receives the most sunlight annually in Japan, and Kitagawara took advantage of these natural conditions, devising spaces that fill with light. The clear skies and dry air intensify the whiteness of the enclosure, adding to the feeling of otherworldliness that the architect aimed to create. The high reflectivity of the facades register the variations in the sunlight and sky, and they change appearance constantly.

The buildings that make up this award-winning complex were designed as a group of "stars" that together form a "constellation." Villa Esterio itself is made up of a series of external passageways that form what seems to be an irrational maze, one that encourages visitors to surrender themselves to chance and sudden surprises—such as suddenly coming across this late afternoon view of light and accented color.

facing page: A single maple tree, chosen for its deep, rich color in the fall, stands radiant in late afternoon sun.

For this three-story house in a suburb of the port city of Yokohama, the client wanted to maximize use of the available space—hence three floors—while retaining an open and airy feeling. In discussions with the architect, Michimasa Kawaguchi, it was decided to follow the model of a central *tsubo-niwa*, but to make this work on all the floors. Kawaguchi specializes in domestic architecture and is in great demand for his knowledge of traditional construction and finishing techniques, which he applies in a modern style. The *tsubo-niwa*, while central, opens out to the front of the house, which both allows more light into what is effectively a deep light well, and provides a garden view when entering. A single maple is planted in a bed of *ryu-no-hige,* or mondo grass (*Ophiopogon japonicus*), surrounded by white gravel. At each level, shoji screens in the design known as *fukiyose* slide back to reveal this central space. The house being deeper than its facade, the screens in the front and rear rooms align so that when open they provide a view all the way through to the back, where a small vertical garden space is planted with tall-growing *mousou-chiku* bamboo. On the first floor, decking and a parapet of cypress make maximum use of this internal, central garden, surrounding the central space on three sides.

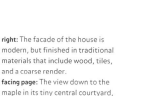

right: The facade of the house is modern, but finished in traditional materials that include wood, tiles, and a coarse render.
facing page: The view down to the maple in its tiny central courtyard, from the top floor.

facing page: The young maple being trained with bamboo supports, seen from the side room with the shoji screens drawn back.

above: *Mousou-chiku* bamboo, a tall-growing Phyllostachys species, in the small rear garden. The design of the shoji screen is known as *fukiyose*.

above left: The garden viewed from the entrance. Leading up to it, the concrete flooring is set with scattered groups of black pebbles in a style known as *hifumi-ishi* (*ishi* means stone; *hi-fu-mi* when written in Chinese spells "one-two-three").

above right: A closer view shows the mondo grass in which the tree is set, known in Japanese as *ryu-no-hige*, or "dragon's beard."

left: On the second floor, shoji screens can be opened to expose the full depth of the house, both for visual effect and to promote air circulation in the hot summers.

Occupying a central light well in a two-story building designed for a jewelry manufacturer, this bamboo garden framed against verdigris copper was designed by architect Atsushi Kitagawara as part of the same wedding center in Kobu city as the Villa Esterio (see pages 14–15). Here curves play a key role, evoking a gentle harmony, suggesting the flow of direction, and promoting a "floating" theme.

The garden, which is intended to represent a blue and green pond, has windows on three sides. One low window facing the building entrance is in the shape of a leaning parabola, a curve that is repeated later in the teahouse on the roof terrace above. Indeed, all the elements of this cool garden are designed to direct one up to the teahouse, where the curved roof recalls the shape of the window as well as the slope of the copper wall. The long, thin bamboo trunks shoot up from a bed of another, dwarf species of bamboo, drawing the eye up through this pocket panorama to the roof. On the upper floor, the bamboo leaves frame the walkway that leads to the teahouse.

below and facing page: The square central garden at the foot of a light well can be viewed from three sides. Here, the upward sweep of the patinated copper backdrop rises from the grass bamboo. The low window next to the main entrance echoes the curve, as does the light entering from another window next to the door.

left and facing page: Conceptually, the garden plays a role in the approach to the teahouse on the roof (just visible at the top left). The bamboo leads the eye upward, and its leaves form a thick canopy for the walkway above.

Architect Denso Sugiura specializes in designing houses on extremely small plots of land in central Tokyo, using tall plants with tiny footprints at the base. Small and awkwardly shaped plots are nothing new in modern urban Japan, where space is at a premium; the usual solutions are claustrophobic, demanding a certain stoicism from residents and an acceptance of limited views. As Sugiura notes, the tendency to pack in as much as possible became even more pronounced during the economic boom in the 1980s, when land prices soared: "The general reaction of most people to the hike in land prices was to fill every square inch and have as many rooms as possible."

The typical plot size that the architect works with is around 320 square feet, tiny even by Japanese standards, and appropriately he calls these house designs *chitchai*, or tiny houses. "Some people—my clients at least—understand the importance of living with a garden space for their own well-being," he says. To that end, he devotes a portion of this valuable space to a central plant that extends up through the floors and becomes part of the dwelling. The choice of tree in the design is essential: it must be suitable for growing up through two or three stories, but occupy a minimum planting area with few, if any, spreading branches.

In the first of the two houses shown, a corner property in Aoyama, the dimensions are 22 by 14 feet, giving an area of just 300 square feet. Here Sugiura chôse a Japanese dogwood, or *yamaboshi*. Its multiple trunks rise up almost parallel through the small square aperture in the wooden ceiling of the first-floor space to branch above the second floor, where the tree is surrounded by a low wooden bench. This species of dogwood, very popular in China and Japan, is hardy, needs little attention, and offers seasonal variety—abundant green leaf cover that turns reddish-brown in fall, followed by berries.

The second property, in Minato, is slightly larger at 430 square feet, but in this case the owners needed to use part of the space for parking. The plant of choice here was bamboo, the thick-stemmed *mosotake* known for its profusion of small leaves. Bamboo spreads readily, so to keep its growth in check the planted area below ground level is encased in concrete. The garden plan is just 9 by 4 feet, slightly smaller than the traditional *tsubo-niwa*.

facing page: In the summer, the second floor of the house in Aoyama opens up fully to the deck, through which the dogwood grows. This is one of fifteen houses designed on similar principles by architect Denso Sugiura.

above left: Through the open front door of the house in Minato, the view continues past Japanese stewartia to a small bamboo plot beyond the open staircase and glass wall.

above right: A narrow light well in the same house allows the *mosotake* bamboo to grow the full height of the three-story building.

above left: Two small openings at the foot of the exterior wall house cubic lights and look through to dwarf azaleas planted on a narrow strip that borders the lane outside.

above right: A textured concrete wall adds interest to the tiny plot, seen here from the traditional tatami room on the ground floor.

right: In the Aoyama house, expanded steel lathing allows air to circulate freely, while the low wooden bench helps to confine the trees branches, in addition to providing a seating area.
facing page: On the ground floor, the slim vertical trunks of a dogwood dominate the white-tiled area, designed for multiple use.

The arced and apparently solid exterior form of this highly unusual weekend house, located near one of Japan's premier surfing beaches at Katsura, about a two hours' drive from Tokyo, belies a completely contrasting interior with three embedded and secluded miniature gardens.

The owner requested privacy and security, and therefore no windows, and wanted a space amenable to her dog, after which the house is named: Borzoi. As has come to be expected from architect Norisada Maeda's considered and always imaginative solutions, the result is unique and surprising, while being entirely functional and comfortable. The exterior, finished in galbarium steel sheets (an aluminium-zinc coating that is about six times more weatherproof than galvanizing), is shaped like a wave to echo those crashing on the shore nearby (Maeda is also an avid surfer). The curve softens what would otherwise be a fortresslike lack of windows.

Inside, however, the contrast is absolute: a white interior with three large light wells, each containing a small, white gravel–floored garden—one at the entrance, another adjoining the living-dining area, and a third at the back where the dog can exercise. The trees in these bright courtyards are Japanese false camellia, which spread into a pyramidal or oval shape; they were deliberately chosen for their similarity to the Indian sal tree, under which the Buddha was said to have been born and which for this reason is often planted at temple entrances.

below left: The folded, slablike exterior, clad with galbarium steel, gives nothing away to passersby, simply marking a very private space.

below right: Seen from the dining area, one of three light wells contains a small gravel garden planted with Japanese stewartia.

A priest's garden in the renowned Gion-ji temple in Mito, northeast of Tokyo, offers an oasis of Zen tranquility. While the two main gardens here are intended for public viewing (one of them a symbolic parable of the Soto sect of Zen Buddhism), this private courtyard is designed primarily for viewing from the quarters of the resident priest.

Gion-ji was established in 1683 by a grandson of Ieyasu Tokugawa, founder of the Edo shogunate, and is one of the most important centers of the Soto sect. Recently rebuilt—the construction was completed by Mikami Architects, and the gardens by Zen priest and garden designer Shunmyo Masuno—the themes of the reconstruction were reticence and strength, conveyed purposefully by the combination of massive, polished concrete and cypress flooring and Masuno's precise and confident placements of stone, green islands, and gravel. The windows facilitate the viewing experience: from the priest's room, screens in *washi* (handmade) paper limit the view severely to the ground, while from the corridor on one side a single sheet of sandblasted glass slides smoothly into a recess in the thick concrete wall.

right: The view from the priest's room is intentionally restricted by the window and ledge to reveal only the surface area of the garden. Shoji screens cover the window.

above and facing page: From the main corridor of the new temple construction, built in polished concrete and with a floor of cypress, a single long window of sandblasted glass opens to reveal a side view of the garden.

The garden devised by Yasoujiro Aoki is central to the experience of this house in Fujiidera, Osaka, designed by his long-standing collaborator, architect Chitoshi Kihara. The house offers three views of the garden from different points: a low-framed one from the entrance, one from the living room on one side, and one from the tea-ceremony room on the other.

The first view is precisely controlled, directing the gaze of the visitor from the entryway toward the ground, though a door to the left opens onto the small square courtyard. Two other openings provide easy access to the garden through sliding screens, allowing guests in the living area to step down and cross the small garden to enter the tea-ceremony room, with its unusual bright red alcove, or *tokonoma*.

A maple tree from the southern island of Kyushu is the principal element here, its branches spreading out from one corner of the garden. Behind a stone path that leads across the gravel, a low opening in the rear wall creates a frame for the plantings behind, backed by a second concrete wall. A stone basin for washing the hands and face (an essential preparation for the tea ceremony) and a *kutsunugi-ishi*, or stone for removing shoes, in front of the tea-ceremony room complete the design.

right and facing page: Two opposing views of the square courtyard garden. At right, it is seen framed by the small entrance to the tea-ceremony room looking toward the living room. On the opposite page, the view from the living room shows the short path that leads to the tea-ceremony room—the formal approach for tea ceremonies.

right: This is the first view of the small garden for visitors as they enter through the front door. As in the priest's garden on the preceding pages, the view of the garden is controlled to concentrate the attention on the lower details.

The Tokyo residential district of Ikedayama has lost its once-famous hillside views of Mount Fuji to development, and so one aim of the design of this new house by young architect Junichi Sanpei was to expand the sense of space and reintroduce nature. A key solution was to adopt a courtyard style that draws in the exterior: all the windows face the courtyard, and full-length glazing of the entrance hall and stairwell further enhances this effect. The use of expanded steel mesh for the sliding front entrance extends the feeling of openness even to the street.

Sanpei created vertical continuity throughout the three floors, which ascend from more public areas to private rooms, using a maple tree planted in the center of the court-yard, tall ranks of bamboo at the back, and a plum tree in the rear corner. A utility room on the top floor leads out to a small roof garden of green lawn, which can also be viewed from the bedroom opposite. The traditional tatami room on the ground floor, occupying an independent space between the courtyard and the separate rear bamboo garden, offers exquisitely framed views through specially designed sliding shoji screens with only horizontal lines.

right: Openness is the theme of this house, and it begins with the view from the quiet street, where a sliding door of expanded steel lathing acts as a window to the two small gardens.

left: A maple tree provides the central focus for the main courtyard. Glass walls on the first two floors help expand the view.

above: The small tatami room is furnished with shoji screens that slide both sideways and vertically to offer a variety of framed views of the garden.

right: From the tatami room, but facing toward the rear of the property, shoji screens at left and *fusuma* sliding doors reveal a stand of bamboo backed by a reed screen wall.

Located in central Tokyo near Roppongi, the main feature of this Japanese-style restaurant, called Tsuki no Niwa, or "Moon Garden," is a striking garden that descends in levels to a carp pond fed with water from a well higher up the slope. The terrace bordered by this rectangular pond is appropriately named *otsukimi dai*, or "moon-viewing place."

Rectangular stone slabs form overlapping tables that carry the water down from the well naturally, guided by strategically placed stones and mounds of small pebbles, and provide a pleasing angular contrast to the loose and informal plantings. In the evening candles are lit in small stone lanterns along the water's course.

Seasonally blooming trees and flowers provide a changing backdrop throughout the year. White and red plum trees blossom and perfume the air in the early spring, followed by the pale purple flowers of rhododendron and white blossoms of the Kousa dogwood in April. Ericaceae flowers in May, and the colorful hydrangea blooms in the rainy season of early summer. In fall, deciduous leaves paint the garden in various colors.

facing page: A long, shallow carp pond borders the foot of the sloping, stepped garden, fed by water trickling from the well above.

above: The final slab of stone on the watercourse was chosen and positioned to allow the water to pour in a series of tiny rillets.

facing page and left: On the upper sections of the watercourse, mounds of gravel and strategically placed stones channel the flow along the overlapping slabs, while small, hollowed-out stone lanterns create flickering reflections.

Architect Michimasa Kawaguchi was responsible for the conversion and extension of this ancient property in Kita-ku, Tokyo, which included an old stone two-story warehouse. Two tiny garden spaces were a gentle addition. One is the area fronting the narrow street, which Kawaguchi planted with *akebono* bamboo for its delicate and light appearance. The stands on either side of the doorway interact visually with the vertical wooden slatting above a low concrete wall cast with a formwork of wooden planking. Inside, the entrance is a subtle conflation of exterior and interior; a young maple holds the center, surrounded by plastered walls and a large single-pane window. The room, which gives access to the old building on one side and the new extension on the other, is paved with blue Izu stones.

below right: Just inside the new entrance, a picture window gives out from a study/dining room onto the small courtyard garden planted with a young maple.

below left: A seventy-year-old stone warehouse stands on the west corner of the property.

above: The facade on the narrow street is a carefully ordered arrangement of wood and plantings. *Akebono* bamboo is integral to the design, complementing the widely spaced wooden slatting behind.

In this house located in Sakai, a once-flourishing port town, Kansai-based garden designer Toshiya Ogino has exercised his characteristically clean lines and minimal plantings to animate three small interior courtyards, choosing for each a single, delicate tree offset in one corner.

The relatively long, shallow courtyard in front of the living room, punctuated by wooden beams, contains a full-moon maple, which spreads its delicate feathery leaves against the simple white wall to maximize the feeling of spaciousness. At its foot is a water basin, or *mizubachi*, of Aso stone, a dark volcanic lava that is quite easy to carve and is highly porous, remaining moist and cooling—a particular favorite of Ogino. Three different bamboo grasses provide ground cover, each a different shade of green.

A glass-enclosed smaller courtyard in the center of the house both acts as a divider and creates continuity between the living room and tatami room. Here a handsome small oak grows from a ground cover of ferns and a mulch of natural bark and sprigs. In the autumn, its acorns help give the impression of woodland, and the view between the two rooms, across the house, is one of nature interspersed with living space.

right: The principal central courtyard, seen here from two sides, provides a linking, planted space for the largely open-plan interior. From the tatami room, the view extends through to the longer, narrower courtyard on the other side.
facing page: From one side, the delicate shape of the oak is outlined against a white wall.

above: A courtyard garden, with decking that runs the length of the living room, is planted with a leaf-fan acer near one corner.

facing page: The third and smallest courtyard garden is by the entrance to the house. It too is planted with a young acer.

In the midst of a large house in Tondabayashi, south of Osaka, a small central courtyard, also the creation of Toshiya Ogino, is similar in function to the green spaces of the Sakai house (see the preceding pages), joining two rooms and providing the illusion of living among the trees. Here Ogino worked with renowned Osaka architect Akira Sakamoto, several of whose minimally white constructions are also featured in this book.

This house furnishes examples of three styles of pocket garden: central, as in this case, as well as edge and image as discussed in the other chapters. Here the off-center siting of the tree in the central courtyard is crucial to the composition, its slender branches spreading from one corner across a bed of moss and an old stone water trough.

facing page: The view across from one main room to another is carefully composed. The tiny courtyard is bounded by opposing glass windows and concrete walls on the other sides.

The courtyard at the center of this house in Kashiba city, close to Nara, provides both space and tranquility for the two families who share this residence. While they can sense each other's movements, the couples (the younger with children) also have the privacy they require to lead their separate lives. The house and its garden are another example of collaboration between Osaka architect Akira Sakamoto and garden designer Toshiya Ogino.

A certain austerity pervades this elegant and largely white space. Three windows look out onto the courtyard: a large window from the older couple's wing, a second smaller one from an interconnecting corridor, and a third low-framed one that presents a severely cropped view from the young couple's side. A white birch's slender trunk harmonizes with the pure white walls. Its leaves turn from vibrant green in summer to a hazy yellow in autumn, adding color. Adjacent to it is an unusually tall, three-sided water basin of volcanic Aso stone, its tapering form making it look as if it is embedded in the special rusted gravel brought in from Isé, where the Imperial Shinto shrines are—in Ogino's imagination, like a meteorite that has impacted the earth.

right: The garden design is fully integrated with the architecture: white birch complements the white walls of the courtyard, while the three-sided stone water basin echoes the asymmetrical arrangement of the garden's three windows.

above and facing page: While the garden can be viewed and accessed from the corridor and the older couple's wing of the house, the low window on this side, where the younger family lives, tightly limits the composition.

Architect Satoshi Okada, known for his unusual innovations and preference for black, designed this striking house on a long, narrow corner lot in Sakakida, in the north of Kyoto. Painted charcoal gray and surrounded by high exterior walls of compressed cement panels, the house and its deep garden ensure privacy. At the same time, the integration of the upper and lower levels via the courtyard space, together with a light well on the second floor, allows both maximum enjoyment of the courtyard garden and a valuable flow of air that cools the house during the hot summer months.

The owner had requested a view of the garden from the bathroom on the ground floor, and from the living and dining area on the upper floor. Mondo grass, an evergreen perennial, provides ground cover for the courtyard's entire length, punctuated by an irregular arrangement of square stepping-stones that lead from a tatami room to the bathroom, and edged by stone and a trough of black pebbles. White enkianthus, which has pretty bell-like blooms in the spring and changes the color of its leaves beautifully in the fall, lends its charm as well. Three different kinds of maple trees add extra delicate shades of color, and their combination of greens and reds are enhanced by the dark backdrop.

To help the residents cope with the summer heat, the courtyard's depth boosts air circulation by creating a temperature difference with a wooden deck above, producing a convectional flow of cool air upward through the entire house.

right and facing page: Bounded by high black walls, the garden has an air of intense privacy. A path of granite stepping-stones connects two of the ground-floor rooms, one a bathroom and the other a tatami room.

right: The tree planted at the corner of the black exterior wall is Kousa dogwood, which is often planted along streets. White flowers blossom in June and eventually produce red berries. The leaves change color in the fall.
facing page: Within the garden, seen here from the tatami room, a small maple surrounded by mondo grass occupies one corner.

Designed by architect Norisada Maeda, this single-story wooden house is based on the mathematical concept of a Klein bottle, a topological space with no difference between the inside and outside surfaces (like a three-dimensional version of the better-known Möbius strip). In Maeda's plan, the exterior and interior aspects of the dwelling flow similarly into one another.

Key to this concept is a long and narrow internal garden, walled in glass, that nearly bisects the otherwise open-plan living space. It reaches the full height of the building, opening to the sky, and accommodates the owner's rather idiosyncratic request that the house appear somewhat like a shop, resembling a display window or showcase.

The floor of the garden is wooden decking, into which palm trees are inserted. Their various shapes, sizes, and sculptural qualities help keep the design simple and clean without seeming too austere. Far from appearing as an enclosed space, the garden, which can be seen from every part of the house, brings the outside in, and in a sense inverts the space. Daylight streams down and radiates out through the gap, and in the evening recessed ceiling fixtures provide illumination.

above and facing page: The courtyard garden is an extremely narrow trough encased in glass, forming a kind of open wall.

This small garden with granite floor, walls, and a water basin is part of a house built slowly by its owner, stonemason and sculptor Masatoshi Izumi, in the corner of the museum and stone yard that he has run for many years. Izumi was a close friend and partner of sculptor Isamu Noguchi, who moved here from the United States for the remaining years of his life (he is buried on an overlooking hill). The Stone Atelier, as it is now known, is a complex of several workshops in the village near Takamatsu, at the foot of Mount Yakuri Goken, where the famous Aji granite is quarried. Aji stone is renowned for its texture, color, and elegant luster. Its fine texture makes it more durable than most granite, and particles of biotite become visible after grinding the stone.

Here, as in the rest of this hand-built house, Izumi has chosen different forms of Aji stone, building the walls by himself in his spare time. This simple, dense but warm space is lit by a single paper lantern of the design made famous by Noguchi. It and the shoji screen on one side of the garden create a philosophical contrast of material opposites with the famous stone, which is used by sculptors and architects across Japan, notably the modern Zen garden designer Shunmyo Masuno.

right and facing page: Paper and stone create a study in contrast. The Akari lantern, in *washi* handmade paper and thin bamboo strips, was designed by the owner's friend and partner, Isamu Noguchi, and became a design icon of the 1950s and 1960s. The wall behind was assembled over time from the local granite that is the source of the stonemason's work.

More familiar to the West are gardens that adjoin dwellings, rather than being enclosed by them. Even more so than courtyard gardens, these have the potential to create a dialogue between the interior and exterior. As noted previously, the interpenetration of outside and inside is a recurring theme in Japanese architecture. In all the examples here, the interface between the house and the garden—whether windows (in various locations and sizes), or sliding doors of glass, or the more traditional paper-on-wooden-frame shoji screens—plays an essential role. These gardens extend the dwelling into the open space, while at the same time creating a buffer against urban surroundings that are often less than attractive. A special type of Japanese "edge" garden derives from the Kyoto tradition of town houses known as *machiya*. These houses, rectangular and very deep in relation to their facade, typically incorporate a long, narrow garden running the length of the property on one side—the term "garden" here including a simple floor of packed earth. The first house in this chapter, for example, translates this very closely into a modern style.

In this terraced house in Tokyo with limited space, architect Michimasa Kawaguchi—in great demand for his sensitive use of traditional materials and techniques in a modern idiom—adapted a solution from an old Kyoto style. Town houses in Kyoto, with narrow facades but great depth, use a passageway along one side, often an earthen-floor "garden," to connect different parts of the property. Although this reduces the width of the house even further, it creates an edge garden that can be accessed from more than one room.

Applying this *machiya* garden, as it is called, to a Tokyo house (the architectural conventions of the two cities are traditionally quite different), Kawaguchi employed a wall of vertical wooden planks separated by single bamboo poles and a flooring of cement set with widely spaced small black stones. The same black stones edge the pathway, where they provide the base for a row of simple plantings. Two thick wooden beams have been placed upright near the entrance, one installed with a tap that plays water onto the concrete and a small circle of stones. The beams are topped with *kokedama*, decorative plants attractively arranged in moss balls that grow around a sticky mulch.

below: The view from the back of the house toward the wooden gate. Scattered black pebbles are set into the concrete floor, in a style similar to that in the house on pages 16–21.

right: A Japanese summer wax tree at the entrance provides seasonal variety, with young green leaves in spring, flowers in late spring to summer, and in autumn, red berries that ripen to black.
facing page: Growing in *kokedama*, ornamental Japanese blood grass decorates the thick wooden blocks that carry the water pipe; the flow of water from the brass tap falls into a circular depression cut out of the concrete floor, filled with pebbles.

Takeshi Nagasaki intended this garden—whose names translates literally to "Garden Now Heaven"— to represent the transience of the present. The property was being rented, so both the client and Nagasaki understood that it would not be used by the same people in the future. Nagasaki interpreted the clients' needs and decided to transform the rooftop into a tranquil place where they could gather with their friends to escape the noise and hectic pace of Tokyo.

Nagasaki introduced a sense of calm, borrowing Zen concepts. The idea for the garden is based on *nure-en,* an open veranda attached to a Japanese house, where people can sit and appreciate the water and the reflection of the moon in it. Here the water is symbolized by the rough surface of the concrete floor, while the shore is conveyed by pebbles at one end. The reflection of the moon is represented three times, by a disk-shaped bronze object and two circular glass lights placed in different spots along the floor. These art objects are part of a series created by Nagasaki, which he calls Direction. Each bears a bamboo impression.

Other adapted Zen techniques include the placement of the Direction objects in a way similar to traditional *tobiishi,* or stepping-stones; the *kakei* (bamboo water spouts) sandwiched between the planks of the wooden deck seating, which carries water away to gently drop and spread ripples in a water basin; *shakkei* (the Japanese interpretation of "borrowed landscape," the gardening technique of framing a distant view to incorporate it into the visual experience of the garden) against the urban background; and different layers of *misugaki* (fencing), employing bamboo loosely spaced to allow partial views through it.

right and facing page: Building onto the existing terrace wall, Nagasaki designed a series of bamboo screens that soften the visual effect of the surrounding Tokyo sprawl. The spacing allows plenty of light to filter through.

right: A bowl of macha—the powdered green tea used in the tea ceremony—accompanied by a traditional sweet (*wagashi*) that takes the edge off the tea's bitterness is enjoyed in this peaceful setting.

above: Wooden seating on both sides of the small terrace is carefully detailed. Green bamboo is laid between the wooden boards, and one functions as a water spout to trickle rainwater into a blue ceramic bowl.

above and facing page: A key feature of the tiny garden is the design of disclike objects that carry the imprint of a bamboo culm. One is in verdigris bronze and the other two are cast glass. Lighting underneath each lends an enchanting strangeness to the garden at night.

Located on the roof terrace of a three-story condominium in Tokyo, this maintenance-free garden is unusually sited right next to the bathroom, where it can be enjoyed through glass walls. Because the owner is away frequently, hardy evergreens—ash and sword ferns—were planted, and are maintained by an automatic watering system. Aquasoil (a fused blend of potassium-based co-polymers) is used for the earth; it is lightweight and retains moisture well, making it particularly suitable for rooftop gardening. Its efficiency allows a thinner cover, rather than the usual soil depth requirement of 1 to 3 feet for planting.

To suit the compact space, the wooden decking is arranged carefully; planks are laid parallel to the building on the narrow sides of the garden but diagonally in the corner to visually enlarge the space. The corner plinth into which the tree is set is lit from within through opalescent panels for a floating effect.

facing page: Vertical boards used for the fencing isolate the garden from the surrounding cityscape, but are spaced to allow the light to shine through. An ash tree occupies the corner.

left: For visual interest and to increase the feeling of space, the decking is arranged at various levels and the planking laid in different directions. Concrete containers and surrounding pebbles add further notes of texture.

above: The bathroom is adjacent to the garden, with the bath positioned next to the plain glass walls for an optimal view.

In a new suburban residential development in Kamishizu, this property has the good fortune to be situated next to a public park, ensuring no high-rise building on that side. To take full advantage of this, architect Junichi Sanpei took the unusual step of raising the house's living area up on piers and devoting half of it to a garden in the form of a pristine lawn that blends visually with the view of the park.

The living, dining, and kitchen areas are arranged in an L-shape along two sides of the square lawn, facing onto it with full-length glass walls. The elevation provides enough privacy to allow this degree of exposure, and the view from the living area extends seamlessly across the park to the trees beyond. A stainless-steel mesh screen walls in the garden's other two sides. In the architect's eyes this green "miniature-scape" recalls the land before suburban development. The lawn also serves as natural insulation for the bedrooms below on the ground floor.

right and facing page: All rooms except the bedroom and utility room are raised on slim steel pillars. The open space beneath is used for parking.

following pages: Nearly half of the upper floor area is given over to a grass lawn, bounded on the two outer sides by a transparent wall of expanded steel lathing, and on the other two sides by a continuous glass wall with sliding doors.

Using old wooden beams and other materials from a 130-year-old farmhouse, architect Ryusuke Fujioka crafted this modern home in Tondabayashi, south of Osaka, for a well-known Kansai artist. The ample dimensions of the original structure are continued in this atelier-cum-dwelling, and the architect chose to exploit this space by fitting floor-to-ceiling glass on the side facing the garden, all of which is raised one level above grade. The view from the living area, where glass doors slide open to extend the space to a wooden deck, takes in the clean lines of the garden, designed by Toshiya Ogino using raked white sand, moss beds, and rough square stepping-stones. The artist's atelier is located on the opposite side.

Ogino chose a sparse planting of pines that echo this area's former forests of Japanese red pine, now largely disappeared due to the incessant Japanese appetite for housing space. The trees include one pine from Shinshu in Nagano prefecture, and another from Noto that sits nearest the street. The latter, with a thicker trunk, leans in toward the house and asserts its presence strongly. To enhance the seasonality of the garden, Ogino added a fast-growing variety of maple close to the house at the other end of the garden. For ground cover, moss, crested leopard plants, and Japanese pachysandra form a strong green base against the fine raked Chinese sand.

facing page: The view from the wall on the street side. The two pines dominate the scene, appearing to rise cleanly through the bed of sand. The main wing of the house is on the left, the artist's studio on the right.

facing page and above: The view from
the living room, looking across to the
wall of the studio with its high windows,
as seen in the afternoon (left) and the
evening (right). The stepping-stones
in front are from a mountain close
to Kameoka, near Kyoto, and known
as *tanbakurama-ishi*. The two seat-like
stone sculptures resemble *pokkuri*,
a type of Japanese sandal.

above: At the rear of the house, low windows reveal another narrow edge garden.

In the appropriately named House of Shadows, in Tokyo, architects Hiromi Koori and Toshiya Endo of Studio MY responded to the client's request of a house that would in some way be different and quieter than the metropolitan surroundings by playing with light — reflections, shadows and chiaroscuro. Key to this is the water garden that runs along half of the length of the building, bridged by an elevated deck on one side and an open metalwork staircase leading down into the garden. Decking leading from the street entrance edges a shallow pond with a tiled base, which step up to a second tiled level that extends to the row of slender bamboos at the end. Wooden beams span part of this open area, adding their pattern of shadows when the sunlight strikes.

right: The play of reflections shimmer in the pool. Its shallowness allows every slight breeze to ripple the surface.
facing page: The view from just inside the street entrance. The pond also acts as a barrier, leading visitors to turn left to enter the house.

In Kyoto's Murasakino district, this deep house with a relatively narrow facade has been defined by the strong rectilinear design of its front and rear gardens. Everything is framed and positioned with precision—the alignment of the massive rectangular white stone slabs that divide the garden at the front; the openings of a low window on the left side of the facade; and the main doorway that continues through to the small tatami room and its shoji screens, which open onto the rear courtyard garden.

Throughout the house, views of the gardens can be opened, closed, or partially revealed. Architect Hiroshi Yoshikawa's reinforced-concrete and steel house works with garden designer Toshiya Ogino's sense of perspective, so that alignments of the two constantly appear and surprise. Two stone water basins, or *mizubachi*—one just inside the low window at the front, the other in the old-looking, mossy, lava-strewn garden at the rear—become focal points for these changing perspectives.

facing page: The view of the small rear garden from the tatami room is carefully composed, as in all of Ogino's designs. Sliding the shoji screens open to different degrees creates a pleasing variety of framings.

right: A low, round, and straight-sided *mizubachi*, or water basin, is sited among fern and moss to give it an old appearance, which contrasts with the evident modernity of the house design.

above left and right: The view from the tatami room on the previous page is extended in depth when the front door slides open, for yet another composition.

facing page: On the other side of the house, a massive *mizubachi* is placed just inside a low opening. This gives two completely different visual compositions, from inside and from outside—for example, the reflection of the sun or the moon can be enjoyed at different times. In the front garden, white stone blocks divide the space.

The space available for this small, hand-crafted patio garden in Kichijouji, a pleasant suburb of Tokyo, was a narrow area right on the street in a quiet neighborhood. Because it is located next to a large park, the question of privacy was not important, but the clients had two stipulations: they wanted a play area suitable for their young children, and they did not want the existing persimmon tree to be cut down.

Designer Takeshi Nagasaki decided on a pale theme for this garden. The low wall for the plant bed is built with a white weathered brick from Australia. As the aspect of the patio is southeast, a second tree was needed for shade in the summer. Nagasaki chose a Crape myrtle, its white flowers continuing the color scheme.

As the patio was likely to receive heavy use by the children, he restricted the plantings here to a curved bed around the perimeter. Once the children are older, the fenced decking will be removed and the planted garden extended. For the perimeter of the house, he constructed a path of cement stepping-stones, some set with shells and glass marbles collected by the children, others with impressions of a fern and of the family's handprints.

left: One of the concrete flagstones used in the pathway, set with objects collected by the children, including seashells and glass marbles.

above: All the planting in this edge garden is next to the sidewalk, bounded by a low wall of white Australian brick that is interrupted by dark volcanic boulders from Oshima. A blue-green color theme was chosen for the plants.

above: The view through the lower gap in the fence to the sidewalk. The lantern was imported from the United States.
facing page: Next to the fence, a fanciful water spout is built into the trunk of a *sarusuberi* (Crape myrtle), bored out to carry the pipe.

Accenting the entrance to this white, minimalist house in Habikino city designed by Akira Sakamoto, two stands of yellow bamboo enliven the access from the street. The palette, as always in the frequent collaboration between Sakamoto and garden designer Toshiya Ogino, is restrained. Pale yellow trunks and light green leaves interrupt the severity of the rectangular facade and sway in the slightest breeze. Ogino's expert touch continues inside, in the sophisticated framing of a single maple tree shown in chapter four on page 179.

facing page: The entrance to the house sits back from the street to allow parking space. The choice of yellow bamboo is a conscious attempt to vary the color palette from the green—and white inside.

By the entrance to the large house in Tondabayashi (see also pages 58–59 and 208–211), the garden designer Toshiya Ogino has used a carefully selected and shaped *hauchiwa-kaede* maple tree (*A. japonicum*) to occupy the framed space of an external corner, bounded by a projecting wood-framed window on one side and deep overhanging wooden eaves on the other. The delicacy of the slim branches and feathery leaves makes a satisfying counterpoint to the angularity of the "frame." Gravel fills the external court, and the tree rises from a bed of moss that has been given an irregular, flowing edge. Cutting the boundary between moss and gravel is a *mizubachi*, or water basin, that has been created from the plinth of a traditional stone lantern.

facing page: The maple interacts with the frame created by the concrete walls and wooden projections in this carefully composed view.

Close to the shores of Lake Biwa, in Shiga prefecture, and set among rice fields, the ample size of this private property provided architect Kan Izue with the opportunity to incorporate a variety of miniature habitats, both inside and out. The principal structure is in concrete, but by deliberately breaking it up into angles, protrusions, and pillars, Izue aimed to create the impression of a complex of buildings, something like a small hamlet.

Part of his concept here is the harmony of contrast, or *in-yo*, the Japanese interpretation of the Chinese *yin-yang*. In this case, the lines of the angular and abrupt concrete structures are softened with plants. This symbolism of male and female principles—as Izue himself puts it quite bluntly, "the garden expresses woman, the house expresses man"—is announced even before entering the property, at the side of the house close to the entrance. Izue has created a recessed angle from the street and filled it with plants: an Iroha maple, soft and yellow-leaved against the severe vertical concrete projections, rises above an equally soft and feathery ground cover of the shrublike *okamezasa* bamboo grass.

left: Flowers in soft focus against the sandblasted glass wall of the main entrance to the house.

above: An elongated triangular plot of land is contained in the angle between the main house on the right and the entrance on the left. Maple and short bamboo grass create a soft, feathery contrast to the house's angular structures.

The narrow strips at the back of two new houses in the outskirts of Tokyo form the location of the Sound Garden and the Garden of Red Direction, both by Takeshi Nagasaki. An Ilex sugerokii (*soyogo*) tree divides the two gardens and connects the views from both sides. One neighbor's garden, partly hidden by this tree, becomes the background scenery for the other neighbor's house, for an intentional *shakkei* effect. *Shakkei,* which first evolved in China, has some of its best-known expressions in the old city of Suzhou.

The inspiration for the Sound Garden came from the clients' favorite piano song titled "The Sound of Water," as well as from their love of jazz and the *shakuhachi,* or Japanese bamboo flute. Water drops were splashed onto the wooden fences and scorched with a blowtorch to embed their marks permanently. The droplets represent musical notation, and their random positions are an analogy for jazz. The bamboo arranged vertically against the fence symbolizes the *shakuhachi.* Held in position by overlapping boards, like a flute in the hands of a musician, it also produces a kind of music when raindrops fall through it to strike the ground.

Here Nagasaki created gardens within a garden. He cast and placed disc-shaped objects that are evolved from the Direction series featured on pages 78–83. While the earlier discs contained the impression of a bamboo, these contain miniature gardens inside, using the *ishigumi* technique (to create scenery using the composition of natural rocks).

right: By embedding rocks in different patterns in the round concrete tables, Nagasaki has created a symbolic miniature garden within the overall long space.

left: In this narrow space, the tabletop compositions are positioned principally for viewing from windows in the rear of the house.

right: A single green bamboo is held in place by bent overlapping boards within the fence, recalling the way a flute-player holds the traditional *shakuhachi*.
facing page: The view at night from one end of the garden, which runs along the rear of the house.

The owners of the Garden of Red Direction invited Takeshi Nagasaki to design it after observing the work he completed for his neighbor (see the preceeding pages). In contrast to the Sound Garden, which was intended mostly to be viewed from the windows above, the clients wished to have a garden that they could use. As there are no windows or doors at the back of the house, a walk-in garden accessible from a path along the side of the house was required. Additionally, the owners wanted to install some art objects, and incorporate their favorite color, red.

The centerpiece of the garden is a table made of red concrete, in which are embedded sculptures by Nagasaki titled *The End of the Bamboo*. The same fence used for the neighbor was extended to this garden to provide a sense of continuity. Bamboo inserted between the planks of the wood deck also link it to the neighbor's symbol of the *shakuhachi,* as do the art objects throughout the garden. The flat concrete steps have the additional function of exhibiting more of the sculptures. At night, the shadows of the Ilex sugerokii (*soyogo*) tree shared with the neighbor project onto the step; the red fruit that falls from it also becomes part of the display and adds to the color theme. The area underneath the steps provides a concealed space for another piece, which is visible only when exiting the garden. The formwork of the concrete flooring is planks of the Japanese cedar, which is also employed for the fence, and its pattern is embedded in the concrete.

The bamboo sculptures echo Nagasaki's earlier works: the Direction series of discs that contain bamboo casts. Bamboo is a favorite in traditional Japanese gardens, both for planting and construction. With these sculptures, Nagasaki is able to inject an element of nature into gardens without having to plant greenery. The bronze objects here were first cast in plaster from one of the Direction discs, then curved strongly at the top. This curve represents the leaning tips of tall bamboo groves and symbolically expresses how bamboo bows beyond the limit of breaking.

right: A hidden bamboo sculpture underneath the concrete path that separates the two gardens is intended to be seen only when visitors are leaving.
facing page: The dark fencing, blackened with a blowtorch, contrasts with the red table and the two bronze sculptures that appear to grow out of it, here spotlit in the evening.

above and facing page: Various forms of
The End of the Bamboo sculpture give
the garden its focus. The starting point
in each case is a cast of bamboo culms,
which is curved and shaped in clay
before being cast.

Mobility and rearrangement are inherent in the traditional Japanese use of space. The principle is embodied in the shoji, a screen of light cedar wood frame over which handmade paper is stretched, and in *fusuma*, solid panels, both of which slide open and closed and can be detached to alter the configuration of interior spaces, or to extend interiors into adjoining gardens.

Yasuhiro Harada, a designer and restaurateur, has applied this changeable allocation of space to Tenchouen, a hugely popular rooftop restaurant in Osaka that overlooks the main river. Rather than merely moving partitions, however, he moves whole rooms and gardens. Guests enter mobile rooms that are on wheels and can be moved around, and the pebble-strewn space between the walkways is occupied by movable garden tray containers. The containers of polished stainless steel are filled with freeze-dried moss and grasses, situated on black pebbles that contrast with the white gravel that covers the terrace—all in the *karesansui*, or dry-stone garden, tradition. The containers are at different heights and of different dimensions, and can be slid and stacked partly over or under each other.

right and facing page: The rectangular containers of polished stainless steel are in different proportions, sizes, and heights. This idea of "mobile gardens" is one that the designer has developed over a number of years.

left: A wooden boardwalk leads around the large roof terrace, connecting the individual rooms and creating a modern version of a stroll garden among the plantings.

Yasuhiro Harada, who designed the rooftop terrace for the restaurant on the previous pages, extended the idea at this restaurant in central Tokyo, part of the Cube chain. The theme of *karesansui*, or dry-stone garden, remains, with only moss to alleviate the austerity, but here Harada plays with the concept. In one corner of the mazelike black-walled restaurant, a private room has an adjoining sculptural complex of stainless-steel trays, each filled with smaller steel containers, with alternating white and black pebbles. Elsewhere, an understair area becomes a half-concealed garden with additional trays of stones, while some of the private rooms—wooden cubes that are nearly individual buildings—feature "gardens" of gravel, pebbles, and driftwood on their roofs. Even the walls incorporate the steel containers, their pebble and moss surfaces seemingly defying gravity.

right: Austere small gardens of gravel and pebbles, some with driftwood, on the roofs of the individual dining rooms are spotlit in the dark space.

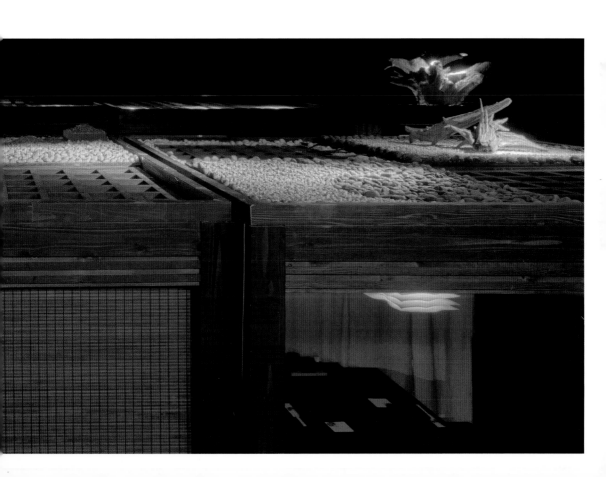

below left, top: One room has within it a private cubic dining room, alongside which is a staggered arrangement of the designer's mobile steel-tray gardens.
below left, bottom: Other tray gardens are half-hidden under the stairs leading down to the lower dining area.
below right: A single tray of white pebbles has *mizubachi* and green bamboo.

below: On one wall, long, narrow stainless-steel containers hold arrays of white gravel and moss.

corner

One of the advantages of garden designs on a small scale is that they can be fitted into spaces that might otherwise be ignored or neglected. As in the houses featured in this chapter, these spaces may be entrances, corners of rooms or patios, and even corners of the building facade. To an extent, this sounds abit like just filling in the gaps, but when planned as part of the integral design of a living space, the result can be much more. These are pocket gardens of the smallest scale, which can be used to punctuate volume and to create points of view at strategic locations. In the case of Device #9, a single-story dwelling, four small gardens, each with its own light well, together articulate the open-plan space. Within the large garden Ryogotei, the designer has embedded a number of tiny individual garden spaces which, in the Japanese stroll-garden tradition of creating points that make the visitor stop, pause, and look, offer miniature compositions to surprise and engage the attention.

In Takamatsu city, the owner of the Takasu Kogei kimono
store commissioned a meditative space in the form of
a large oval room with earthen walls. Rooms designed with
a spiritual or meditative purpose, including tea-ceremony
rooms, also demand some form of transitional space from the
worldly exterior. For this purpose, architect Shinii Kagawa
constructed a miniature garden with undulating blocks of
the Aji granite for which Takamatsu is famous, playing with
the idea of hard stone forming gentle mounds, like moss
or earth. Short stalks of bamboo inserted in the spaces
between the blocks serve as holders for irises. In the corner,
a ceramic water basin of Shigaraki wood-fired stoneware—
one of the oldest pottery styles in Japan—contains floating
camellia flowers.

above: Looking back to the cobblestoned
interior garden from the meditation
room, through a small opening.
facing page: The undulating surface
composed of cubic granite blocks
softens the effect of the rough stone
and adds a sense of flow.

The town of Omihachiman, close to the eastern shore of Lake Biwa, became famous for the manufacture of *kawara*, traditional Japanese clay tiles. An old factory in the historic part of town was scheduled for demolition, but public outcry at a proposal to replace it with high-rise apartments led the city council to plan a *kawara* museum instead. Architect Kan Izue won the design competition.

Izue's aim here is for visitors to experience the three Zen states of the *shin-gyou-sou* aesthetic—literally, "formal softer free"—as they walk through the sections of garden that link the buildings. Geometric patterns and constructions of the old tiles, placed with precision against and in front of white walls, convey the "hard" formality of *shin*. Various green plants, including grasses and feathery bamboo, are employed as a transitional device in the "softening" process, as the visitor proceeds through the outdoor space. The tiles encourage close inspection, creating focal points for the consideration of detail.

right: A row of black bamboo contrasts texturally with the geometric arrangement of the old baked tiles.

In a residential neighborhood an hour outside of Tokyo stands Toko no Ie, which translates as House of Transparent Light. Architect Manabu Miyama's use of volume and space has created an open-plan home that gives the owners the feeling of being outdoors even when they are inside.

The site is awkward and narrow, extending east to west, but Miyama has concealed this constriction by placing Japanese cedar board in a reticular and diagonal pattern. The east-facing entrance opens on to a terrace surrounded by the most striking feature of the design—a facade of translucent, corrugated, polycarbonate panels. This furthers Miyama's theme here of harmony with nature by providing a bright and crisp backdrop, which in the sunlight is adorned with the soft shadows of the leaves and branches of the trees in front of the house. Seen from within, the shifting chiaroscuro pattern of sunlight and shadows against the panels hints at a greater outdoors. At night, the lighting in the interior transforms the panels to produce a glowing lantern effect.

The house's structural scheme, an extensive use of diagonal trusses, is recalled in the plantings on the terrace and in the diagonals of the corner. Two triangular openings in the polycarbonate wall also bring the greenery surrounding the house inside.

right: At night, the lighting in the interior transforms the panels to produce a glowing lantern effect.

left: The house's structural scheme, an extensive use of diagonal trusses, is recalled in the plantings on the terrace and in the diagonals of the corner. Two triangular openings in the polycarbonate wall also bring the greenery surrounding the house inside.

The architectural simplicity of form of this house in
Habikigaoka, in the Kansai region, is punctuated by a
series of individual garden compositions, including framed
miniatures. The designer, Toshiya Ogino, has worked
with architect Akira Sakamoto several times, and the two
complement each other well. Here the color palette for
the garden is minimal—principally green and gray against
the white structure of the house. Trees, all chosen for
their slender profiles, occupy corner positions at the
entrance and in the main courtyard inside; they include a
Chinese ash and Oriental paperbush. Elsewhere, stone
water basins provide the focal point for tiny arrangements
of moss and gravel, framed by low windows at the end
of corridors.

right: A single *toneriko* tree, or Japanese
ash, alleviates the severe minimalism of
the bare facade, which acts as a canvas
for its shadow.

above, right, and facing page: Three views of the small garden behind glass in the entrance area. The hand-carved square *mizubachi* is aligned to the rectilinear design of the architectural elements. Reflections on its perfectly circular depression are a key part of the composition. The rippled edge of the moss softens the lines of the frame. The shrub is a *mitsumata*, sometimes known as Oriental paperbush, one source of handmade paper.

right: In the main courtyard, a similar elegant simplicity reigns, with young maple trees providing the verticals that divide an arrangement of raised wooden decking and lawn. The designer chose plain grass as a play area for the family's young child.

Ichirin is a fashionable restaurant located in the basement of a building in the Akasaka entertainment district of Tokyo. Private Japanese-style dining rooms line a narrow stone-paved corridor, raised so that diners must step up into them, after having first shed their footwear on the *kutsunugi-ishi*, a stone placed for this purpose. At floor level, a series of miniature gardens has been created, tucked into edges and corners, and even running underneath the raised rooms, illuminated with specially designed lanterns. For most customers, these gardens are a peripheral experience, barely noticed on the way to dine. But for those who care to pause, crouch down, and look, they present tiny landscapes of rocks, ferns, and mosses that testify to a high level of attention to detail.

below: One of the private dining rooms is partly cantilevered out, and in the space underneath rocks and ferns comprise a low hidden garden.

above: Every possible space is utilized for garden compositions, including the narrow strip adjoining the step leading up to the kitchen.

At the end of the principal ground-floor corridor in this house near Nara (see pages 60–63 for its central courtyard), by Akira Sakamoto and Toshiya Ogino, a pair of silver birches are arranged to be viewed from different vantages—one, which occupies its own small courtyard, from within the house, and the other, outside, from the street. One of the slim trees, a white birch, occupies a small individual plot bounded on the inside by a plain sheet of glass and on the outside by a steel mesh grille. Just outside, the second similar tree draws the eye inward to this precisely defined pocket garden.

right: The view at the end of the main corridor that runs the length of the house. The silver birch is contained behind a glass wall.
facing page: The same tree seen from the exterior, partly framed on the left by a second silver birch planted along the edge of the sidewalk.

Like many new residential areas in Japan, this fashionable neighborhood in Ashiya city, close to Kob by the Inland Sea, was formerly a forest. Designer Toshiya Ogino, working here with architect Kazuhide Asao, was determined to plant reminders of the pine trees that formerly covered this hillside. However, the areas available for planting were only around the margins of the property, and the architect wanted to maintain the purity of line of the structure. Accordingly, Ogino opted for isolated plantings in the corners. Two Japanese red pines at the front stand tall and straight, matching the vertical lines of the facade. At the back, Ogino planted a soft Japanese ash to fill the restricted space, which grows by a stone water basin. Although the space is narrow, the vertical lines of this slim and beautiful tree prompt the viewer to look up toward the open sky—a recurrent device in the designer's work. Slabs of dark stone form a stepping-stone walkway around the house.

facing page and above: A slender Japanese
ash gently fills the narrow space at
the rear of the house, rising next to a
rectangular water basin.

right: The rough dark slabs of stone from Mount Aso form a pathway around the house, providing a textural contrast to its smooth white and glass structure.
facing page: Interlocking joints add interest to the arrangement.

Down a winding stone path flanked by azaleas and rhododendron lies the entrance to one of the largest private gardens in the country, located in Japan's second city, Osaka. Garden designer Masatoshi Takebe has employed his unique talents here to produce a fusion of Japanese and English styles.

While the garden is most notable for its size—more than 100,000 square feet—and spectacular plantings that include highly prized red azalea, among fifty other varieties, it also has the more subtle pleasures of the traditional stroll garden. A winding pathway takes the visitor on a varied journey through different styles of planting, by ponds and across stepping-stones, and at every turn Takebe has embedded miniature scenes that work independently of the whole. Updating the Japanese tradition, he has also employed a variety of stones, both natural and cut, as vehicles and focal points for particular groupings. These include a curiously shaped water basin with cut indentations, stepping-stones that lead through moss and grasses to a tea-ceremony room, and columnar basalt.

facing page: Japan's complex geology makes it rich in a variety of stones, particularly volcanic and metamorphic. These hexagonal pieces of columnar basalt have an almost man-made appearance.

left and above: An intricate composition of stepping-stones, including one rectangular slab with a scallop-cut edge, has a branch leading to a tatami room. A typical Japanese garden strategy for placing stones is to site them across boundary lines, such as between moss and gravel.

right: A boat-shaped water basin rests in the middle of a small stream.

In a small temple hidden in the heart of downtown Kyoto, the living area for the priest, Hitoshi Akino, and his wife included a backyard, which had no purpose other than to house the outdoor toilet. When the outhouse was destroyed in the Kobe earthquake of 1995, architect Terunobu Fujimori devised a modern teahouse to replace it, including the customary approach—the pathway and garden that prepare the visitor for the experience.

While the teahouse is of course the main feature, the space that precedes it is of huge importance, and is often overlooked in the Western understanding of the ritual and philosophy of the "way of tea." Upon entering here, the visitor follows the *roji*, or path, and leaves the mundane behind. A key stopping point, which demands attention, is the *tsukubai*, or stone washbasin, where the visitor kneels to wash face and hands in a humble ritual cleansing, a reminder of the Buddhist origins of the tea ceremony. The small landscape around the *tsukubai* is always worthy of study and appreciation. In this little corner, Fujimori has embedded the stone basin—specially chosen and milled out for this purpose—in black pebbles that represent a deep, still pond, surrounded by the austerity of white gravel.

right: An arrangement of stones includes an unusual water basin—a circular depression carved into a natural and low-profiled boulder. The black pebbles symbolize a pond within the surrounding white gravel.

This two-story house in Kuritani, Kanagawa prefecture, south of Tokyo, is built on two levels because of the slope of the site. The design, by Ken Architects, combines two very distinct architectural styles—Japanese and Western.

The principal entrance at street level is Japanese; a second, and larger, entryway to the upper level features a Western style. As a connecting device, the architects introduced a shaft in the form of a light well that extends through both levels and planted within it two thick-stemmed bamboos. From the Japanese entrance on the lower level their green stalks are prominently framed, set among white pebbles between low *nanten*, or heavenly bamboo, and illuminated by strategically placed lighting. From the upper level the tops of the bamboo are visible, with the leaves prominent, and they complement an array of thin stainless-steel pillars that help define the entrance.

right and facing page: Two views at different elevations of the same pair of bamboo: at right, from the Western upper-level entrance, next to a screen of stainless-steel pillars; and at far right, the recessed base in the Japanese-style entrance on the lower level.

Located at the end of a blind alley in a crowded residential area in Tokyo, this narrow house makes an unusual visual statement. With barely room for planting, a tall gatelike construction in front is topped with a stainless-steel container garden.

The garden's designer, Satoru Masaki, is an expert in giving traditional Japanese plantings a new twist in modern settings—one of his previous gardens incorporated the trees and plants associated with Japan's original national religion, Shinto, into a private residential space. Here the entire structure echoes the well-known *torii* gates located at the entrances to shrines. He has chosen pampas grass in place of the more common Japanese silver grass, both for its hardiness and—for Tokyo—its exoticism. Elevating the large container makes it prominently visible from the main living areas of the house, particularly at night, when it is spotlit.

right, facing page, and following pages:
Daytime and evening views of the striking structure.

The four meticulous inner gardens of this Chiba prefecture house, named Device #9, intentionally dominate the internal landscape, both physically and spiritually. The wheelchair-bound owner told architect Norisada Maeda to throw away the rules when it came to designing his home. His only request was to create a minimalist, bright open space where nature flowed easily into the enclosed areas.

Maeda's inspiration comes from Ryoan-ji, a famous temple in Kyoto. In the box-shaped house, four simple gardens act as a device to draw in natural light. Stainless-steel boards are used for the garden floor, and reflect the blue skies, clouds, sunset, the moon, and stars.

Lines of water run down on the tilted glass just like raindrops falling on a windshield, making them dance and glitter. The use of tilted glass brings the clients into close contact with nature, and provides a constant but ever-changing panorama. "We can sense the wind by looking at trees blowing in our garden," says the owner. When it is snowing, the house turns into a white world. At night, the garden lights up. All this makes the appreciation of the elements more powerful, and contributes to the stress-free environment.

right: A row of four small conifers, enclosed by glass as if in a display case, faces the entrance at the end of the garage. The bedroom, fully visible, lies beyond.

left: The facade of the building—a single-story, plain rectangular block—with the entrance door (which also doubles as garage door) slid open.
.

preceding pages, right, and following pages: Each of the small corner gardens has its own light well. The floors are all polished stainless steel. The sloping glass walls are designed to catch the raindrops.

image

Gardens of small size can be taken in at a single glance, in their entirety. This simple fact of scale has inspired a number of designers to create gardens as images, framed in such a way that they are organized graphically for viewing. The best are true works of art, installations that use gardening as a creative vehicle. Like other artworks, they balance form and content to varying degrees.

In some of the gardens in this section, the elements of plants, stones, rocks, created structures, and lighting are used primarily for graphic and compositional effect. In others, symbolism and metaphor take prominence, with elements representing ideas as diverse as Buddhist concepts, man's relationship with nature, dualism, myths, heaven, and the underworld.

In this house in Habikino, near Osaka (also featured on pages 108–109), designer Toshiya Ogino, working in concert with architect Akira Sakamoto, has created a study in two-dimensional framed composition. With the shoji doors slid fully back, the square doorway of the traditional tatami room provides the frame for this garden view, while a gently curving white wall some six feet beyond acts as the canvas. Against this background, Ogino has positioned a maple tree that leans in toward the frame, slanting from a specially created slope covered with ferns. The curve of the freestanding wall serves two purposes: it creates a subtle shading across the "picture" seen from inside the room, and adds a sculptural quality to the garden when approached from the outside, continuing the curve of the ground slope.

right: The curved white wall provides a backdrop for the scene on the opposite page, and at the same time contains a second small garden behind.
facing page: Here, the designer's intention is to suggest to the viewer that the space beyond the door continues endlessly to the right, hence the slope of the ground and the slanting tree. The curvature of the wall further adds to the ambiguity of the spatial dimension.

It is common for Japanese gardens to be made of limited materials and to employ a simple color scheme, as is the case with this Kyoto house, where a striking garden is a highly controlled study in minimalism that uses neither flowers nor trees. This modern, three-story dwelling designed by Hisanobu Tsujimura, a rising star of Japanese architecture, was created for a retired couple who share his feeling for simplicity and the appropriate use of natural materials. Part of the inspiration came from the functionalism and rectilinear style of American Shaker buildings, and part from primitive works of art.

Symbolism plays an important role for Tsujimura, as does the interface between interior and exterior. While the lawn and cherry tree on the main side of the house are intended for more conventional enjoyment, this small garden adjacent to the master bedroom is designed for viewing. It is intended to be visible from two perspectives: one from a standing position, and the other, which includes the stone wall, from the bed. Along the wall, lobate curves of moss form soft islands in a sea of white gravel. The garden's name, Tsui-no-sumika, means "last dwelling place," as the couple intend it be their final home.

right: Two repeated curves of moss against white gravel are precisely bounded in the view from the master bedroom.

left: From the level of the bed, the wall is added to the frame of the view.
above: The structure of the garden is illustrated in a side view not intended to be seen.

The Nara house, by Akira Sakamoto and Toshiyo Ogino (see also pages 60–63 and 146–147), contains a garden view of exquisite simplicity, framed from the tatami room that holds the family shrine. An eccentrically placed tree and minimalist composition of moss and gravel occupy a 3-foot-wide space between the threshold of the room and the outer plain white wall. The arrangement is enhanced by a single spotlight aimed from ground level just out of frame to the left; it casts a raking beam across the gravel and the moss that ends in a glowing hemisphere of light, conjuring up the impression of a silent landscape in the moments before sunrise.

right: Recalling the framed view on page 179, the narrow space outside this tatami room where the family shrine is kept is converted by careful composition and lighting into a seemingly larger landscape that flows to the left.

The flowers and trees at the entrance to this apartment block in Osaka were selected for their scent, so that when the wind blows people can enjoy their fragrance. Although the space available was limited, owner-architect Naoto Murata wanted to create as much as possible the feel of walking through nature. Garden designer Toshiya Ogino accordingly planted only along the exterior corridor on one side of the building, but gave prominence to a carefully framed and lit composition at the entrance.

The first glimpse of the composition upon entering shows a tiny rock garden that is recessed because of the frame in the concrete wall, the formwork for which was done in wooden planking for a softer, more natural appearance. The boat-shaped stone on the right is a prized (and expensive) example of volcanic lava from Mount Aso, one of the world's largest active volcanoes, on the southern island of Kyushu. Holding a variety of tiny plants among its crevices and natural vesicles, the stone is lit from above and behind with concealed spotlights. Lava rock absorbs a great deal of water, which makes it good for plants. In this case, it also helps cool the entrance in Osaka's hot summers, as the water evaporates when breezes blow through the rectangular opening, in a natural form of air-conditioning.

Along the side of the building, a few carefully selected trees emerge from behind concrete pillars. Prominent is an Oriental paperbush—the bark of which is used in the production of Japanese *washi* paper—planted in the corner; the visual dynamics change when the tree flowers in spring. The other planting is a winter daphne, which provides a lovely strong scent.

below and facing page: A carefully selected volcanic boulder provides the centerpiece for the framed view at the entrance to the apartment building. By concealing part of the stone at the right, so that it seems to be entering the frame and moving left, the designer adds dynamism to the composition.

right: Along the side of the building, a few carefully selected trees emerge from behind concrete pillars. Prominent is an Oriental paperbush—the bark of which is used in the production of Japanese *washi* paper—planted in the corner; the visual dynamics change when the tree flowers in spring. The other planting is a winter daphne, which provides a lovely strong scent.

This balcony garden, named Ambiguous Space, in the middle of Tokyo was created to reflect the simple and natural lifestyle that the clients aspire to. They had requested a miniature garden for viewing that would be understated and yet offer a scene of which they would not tire.

To address the difficulties of growing plants on a balcony, and the building regulations which precluded the use of soil, designer Takeshi Nagasaki used nonliving, low-maintenance materials, borrowing from nature. He employed the technique of *mitate*—the art of reusing old objects in a new way—to create the feeling of nature, without necessarily its substance. For example, the layered stalks of black bamboo together with the white pebbles underneath inspire an impression of trees in white snow. Cube lights designed by Nagasaki placed among the stones further fuel the fantasy of a night scene. Aiming to create objects that harmonize with the surrounding space—here the top of the lights is a counter-image of the material underneath—he used pebbles in the metal mold into which the glass was blown.

The successful blend of the traditional *karesansui,* or dry-stone garden, with the contemporary urban design contributes to the creation of this "ambiguous" space, which intentionally embodies the Japanese sense of *wabi-sabi*, the complex concept often translated as the beauty of the imperfect and impermanent.

right: One of the specially created cubic lights, sited within the symbolic "forest" of cut black bamboo and surrounded by white pebbles.

left and above: Seen in the context of the apartment, the two balcony spaces appear very restricted indeed, which is why the designer chose to create scenes to be viewed rather than areas to be entered.

above: The cubic lights are a key element. The deep indentations on their surface come from the very pebbles that surround them, which were placed in a metal mold when the glass was blown.

above: Another element is the stainless steel used asymmetrically for the containers. Reflections of the pebbles and lights in their surfaces help to expand the space visually.

Takeshi Nagasaki also designed this balcony garden, next door to the one featured on the preceding pages. This client's particular wish was to have a garden for appreciating the moon, but like the neighbor's balcony, the small space allowed little room for real use. Nagasaki's interpretation—a "floating" garden called Space above Cloud—transformed it into an art-and-garden installation for viewing instead.

Nagasaki carved small, pale gray granite cubes into a craggy surface in the *kobudashi* style, a traditional technique used in building stone walls, and laid them interspersed with flat tiles to produce a checkerboard pattern (known as *ichimatsu*) to represent a cloud. The increasing irregularity of the rough-hewn blocks on the left-hand side implies the movement and dissipation of the cloud as it drifts from right to left.

Another feature of this garden is his design of glass cube lights on the ground, which form the inverse shape of the blocks, and which were made with the same technique described previously: the rough granite formed the base of the cast into which the glass was blown. The horizontally tied bamboo fencing, or *misugaki,* which has the appearance of blinds, marks the boundary between outside and inside without completely shutting out the city. A potted Japanese maple in one corner has been trained and pruned to match the vertical and horizontal geometry. The pot is sunk into part of a granite block to adapt it to the surroundings, and which gives the illusion of it growing from the "cloud." In this way, each element in the composition complements the other.

facing page: On the left side of the balcony, the several elements of the garden blend perfectly, including the granite-block flooring, cube light, bamboo fencing, and maple pruned so that its lines follow the geometry of the overall design.
below: The intricate method of tying the horizontal bamboo poles is detailed.

below and right: Interspersing rough-hewn granite blocks with others that are cut flat in a checkerboard composition is intended to simulate a passing cloud in the sky. The cubic lights hold the impression of the granite blocks on their surface, in a technique similar to that used for the fixtures in the balcony garden on the previous pages.

Ken Architects, who designed and built this 2005 detached house south of Tokyo, in Kanagawa prefecture, had to deal with an existing steep slope, and employed Takeshi Nagasaki to implement a garden that would have a Western aspect from the main house entrance at the top, and a Japanese aspect from the lower level, where a tatami room was built. It is not uncommon in Japan for Western-style houses to incorporate tatami rooms, and the garden in this project needed to address both styles.

Nagasaki handled this requirement by installing a miniature landscape at the foot of the slope, while the rest is covered in grass to form a smooth green wall when viewed from below. The installation comprises two overlapping oxidized-iron sheets resting on stones. From above, only the geometric surfaces of these sheets can be seen, but they also play an important role in defining the surface of the slope. From the tatami room, the space beneath reveals itself to be a cave, with an interior too dim for the eyes to penetrate at first sight. Borrowing from Chinese mythology and well-known in Japanese lore, it represents a hermit's cave on Horai-san, an inaccessible and idyllic mountain island located on a turtle's back in the eastern sea. The slope rising above the cave symbolizes Horai-san itself, while the run of small stones beneath connote the shore of the sea where the turtle swims. From the tatami room, an idiosyncratic design of sliding doors of hand-made paper stretched over a light wooden frame (*yukimi-shoji*) that is raised vertically allow views of the cave-garden and grass slope.

left: The view from inside the tatami room, with the shoji screens slid back. The shadowy interior of the "cave" reveals itself only when the viewer's eyes have had time to adjust to the darkness.

left and below: The steel-topped symbolic hermit's cave, seen from the level of the house's upper entrance, and from the side just in front of the tatami room.

This small austere Zen garden, unusually located on the roof of a condominium within sight of fashionable Roppongi Hills in central Tokyo, is part of a tearoom and garden complex in the sukiya architectural style created by Zen priest and garden designer Shunmyo Masuno. There were many restrictions to overcome in the design, as the garden needed to be crafted within the confines of an urban terrace.

Masuno calls this first garden in the complex, which occupies an entire large penthouse, Muso-tei. The name comes from the Zen word meaning that a person's true identity is ephemeral, and this underlying philosophy links seamlessly to Ueda, the samurai-style tea ceremony, around which the complex is designed. This garden has the function of giving the visitor time to dispel thoughts of the urban surroundings, before moving on to the tea ceremony.

To create the necessary feeling of infinity and serenity, Masuno combined light-colored stones, carefully placed, with white sand. The stone, with a partly cut flat surface, looks as if it has been sliced with a sword, in keeping with the samurai principle. Using cut stone in a Zen garden is unusual and nontraditional, a style introduced by Masuno, the most famous modern interpreter of Zen gardens. A bamboo fence around the perimeter creates a peaceful enclosure, drawing the line of sight upward to the sky. In this garden, the chaos and traffic of central Tokyo below seem to no longer exist.

right: Part of the principal stone in the composition has been cut away horizontally and then polished, an oblique reference to a samurai's sword.
facing page: The arrangement of islands of stone and moss in a sea of raked white gravel, counterbalanced by two heights of bamboo fencing, is both elegant and thoughtful, and repays long study.

In addition to the Zen rooftop garden featured on the preceding pages, this luxury condominium located in Minami-Azabu, in the center of Tokyo, also has an entrance garden by designer Shunmyo Masuno. Masuno, a Zen priest whose family temple is in Yokohama, wanted to re-create the sanctuarylike feeling of a temple approach, which generally has three gates—at the south, west, and east. The temple symbolism is of passage, bringing the visitor closer to nirvana.

A flow of plants and rocks proceeds in shallow curves from the street on the east side, guiding the visitor until it turns off to end along one side of the building, where it forms a sheltered, framed garden, offering a composition of harmony and tranquility that is designed to dispel thoughts of the city beyond. Viewed from inside the lobby, the quintessential Japanese combination of rocks, pebbles, and sculptured plantings is framed through a single glass pane that cuts off the view at the top to exclude the neighboring street and buildings; the sense of flow from outside is achieved by the diminishing sequence of rocks and the fingers of low shrubs, the two forming an arc over the pristine bed of small stones.

right: One of this designer's favorite treatments of stone is a contrast between rough and polished surfaces. Here, through laborious stonework, the two textures flow into each other.

below: A succession of stones from the street entrance come to a halt next to the lobby, from where it can be seen as a framed composition, partly enclosing a sea of gravel.

This house in Tondabayashi, previously featured in chapters one and two (see pages 58–59 and 110–111), also has two gardens designed with symbolic imagery. In the central courtyard, Toshiya Ogino focused the composition on two large flat stones that represent the sun and crescent moon, and also form part of the path of stepping-stones across the white gravel and moss that link the rooms. The symbolism is reprised in an inverted form in a small stone near the entrance to the house, where the same motif is carved into its surface as two water-filled depressions.

On another side of the house, a garden area is accessed from a large tatami room by means of traditional shoji sliding screens. Here a magnificent pine symbolizes connections to the past through its exposed roots, which rise up from a carefully sculpted mound of moss and stones surrounded by white pebbles.

facing page: The same motif of a sun with an adjoining crescent moon is continued in a stone water basin by the entrance to the house.

left: An undulating path of stepping-stones that connects two wings of the house across the courtyard garden becomes, in the middle, a sun and crescent moon.

below and facing page: In contrast to the designer's many asymmetrical compositions, the traditional theme of this house and garden, intended to foster a sense of age and history, encouraged a more formal design treatment. In both these key views from within tatami rooms, the trees are presented as centered elements when the shoji screens are drawn back.

Architect Ichirou Sato's design for Kawano Hotoride, a restaurant in the Aoyama district of Tokyo, demonstrates how seamlessly traditional style has evolved into modern Japanese design.

In the basement of a building, an 80-foot artificial river runs through the center of the restaurant, dividing the dining room in half, with a bar on one side and private rooms on the other. The overall style is traditional, but Sato's clean lines and contemporary twist make a modern statement. Each room is named after a tree or a plant. The river is stocked with about fifty *kawamutu* fish, which are constantly fed to keep them in view of the customers.

While the stream is real, the plants that change with the season are artificial, though deceptively authentic-looking: in spring the restaurant is full of cherry blossoms, in the summer with vivid greenery, and in fall the leaves are yellow and red. The stones in the river are a mixture of real ones, placed along the path and bridge, and manmade versions, which edge the stream.

right and facing page: Autumn is represented by the famous Japanese *momiji*—maples in rich fall colors.

right: In summer, the color theme is green, this time with real plants situated along the flowing stream.

left: Spring means cherry blossoms, some of them strewn on the bridge that crosses to the private dining rooms.

Shinobu-tei, a restaurant in the same group as Kawano Hotoride (see the preceding pages) located in the entertainment district of Akasaka in Tokyo, is built around a convincing representation of a Zen temple garden. Three stones, manmade but realistic, of different shape, size, and height are carefully sited in the basement entrance, two levels below grade. Diners pass by them before entering, and tables on two sides of the garden present different views of the grouping. The composition with one upright stone is classical, as are the surrounding meticulously raked pebbles, intended to represent waves lapping at the shore of an island in the ocean—themes prevalent in Japanese culture and design. This type of garden, composed of just rocks and sand, gravel, or pebbles, is called *karesansui*, meaning literally "dry mountain water," and is defined by a lack of plants. The stones alone serve to convey an image of nature and the landscape. The modern touch of spotlighting (which is never done in temples) gives the garden an otherworldly feel.

right: A monolithic rock arrangement, encircled by a severe and precise raking of white gravel, dominates the exterior at the lower level of the restaurant.

A young couple in a newly built house in a Tokyo suburb asked designer Takeshi Nagasaki to complete their small courtyard garden. The site was above a garage space, making water drainage an issue, and so to ensure this would not pose a problem the floor was sunk to the level of the drain outlet. This move inspired the designer to work with the theme of the underground.

As in the cave garden (see pages 200–203), Nagasaki exercised the principle of *in-yo*, the Japanese interpretation of the Chinese *yin-yang,* in which everything can be divided into opposites of light and dark. Each depends on the other for its existence, and harmony is possible only when the *ki*—the natural energy or vital force that permeates everything— of both is balanced. In addition, the Japanese have a special love of shadow, as famously described in the short classic by writer Junichiro Tanazaki, *In Praise of Shadows*.

To symbolize the world of brightness, Nagasaki used pale cream concrete for a flooring space of overlapping discs. A horizontally spreading Chinese juniper added a touch of nature without unnecessary verticality. Indeed, the lack of height in the garden draws the viewer's gaze down toward the ground level and below, where the world of darkness is symbolized— the mythological underworld. According to *in-yo*, the *ki* of this shadow world creates its antithesis above ground, a world of sunlight and brightness.

Another theme of this garden is infinity, represented by the overlapping concrete discs in the floor. These individual forms suggest endlessness, and the arrangement reinforces the idea of the infinite. They evolved from the designer's original art objects called Direction, and which in earlier iterations contained the impression of bamboo stalks, to symbolize the progression of life. Removing this from the discs here emphasizes infinity, and gives the garden its name, "Garden without Direction." One further design element takes the form of slabs of blue Teppei slate, laid vertically into the earth and stone flooring, to suggest a dragon.

facing page: Slabs of blue-green slate are inserted vertically into concrete and cross the area between a small disc and the ground.

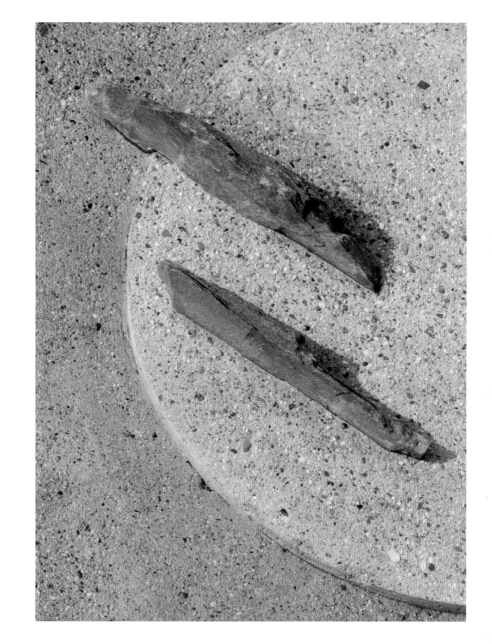

facing page, above, and following pages:
Four overlapping concrete discs launch
outward from the pavement that borders
the garden, partly hiding beneath them
an obscure landscape of rocks. Light and
shade, revealed and concealed, comprise
the theme of this garden.

Featured Architects and Garden Designers